120 EXERCISES
TO BUILD SPIRITUAL
AND FINANCIAL STRENGTH

William and Carolyn Hines

authorHOUSE™

1663 LIBERTY DRIVE, SUITE 200
BLOOMINGTON, INDIANA 47403
(800) 839-8640
WWW.AUTHORHOUSE.COM

© 2005 William and Carolyn Hines
All Rights Reserved.

No part of this book may be reproduced, stored in a retrieval system, or transmitted by any means without the written permission of the author.

First published by AuthorHouse 04/29/05

ISBN: 1-4208-0576-2 (sc)

Library of Congress Control Number: 2004098062

Printed in the United States of America
Bloomington, Indiana

This book is printed on acid-free paper.

Why we wrote this book...

"Wealth gotten by vanity shall be diminished: but he that gather by   labour shall increase."

Proverbs 13:11

We wrote this book because of our sincere wish for everyone to be in a position to obtain spiritual and financial strength..."Money Muscle"...especially to avoid making the mistakes we've made!

Also, in our work with our wonderful client groups, we have been encouraged to share this information.

So, here it is!

> **"The Lord your God gives you the ability to produce wealth, and so confirms His covenant."**
>
> **(Deuteronomy 8:18)**

> **"He became poor so that you through his poverty, might become rich." (2 Corinthians 8:9)**

Are you really serious about keeping more of your hard-earned money? Is your money working for you? Does your month outlast your money? Do you have friends or family members whose month outlasts their money? Do you feel unduly stressed about where your money is going? Do you suffer from "gondoitis?" (I'm "gon-do" better about managing my money!) Are you waiting for "Round-Tuits?" (I'm going to do better about saving / investing when I get "round to it"!) Are you overcome by events or circumstances that drain your spiritual and money resources? Do you want to "walk-the-talk" (act in better accord with your values or beliefs) with personal money matters? Are you an excellent role model for children and others concerning both spiritual and money matters? Do you acknowledge God as the true owner of everything?

Responding to these questions raises challenging considerations for building money muscle or financial strength. We must face these challenges daily. Just like any other physical fitness program you decide to pursue for success, you must be disciplined, organized, unwavering, persistent and positive spirited.

Remember the basic rule for improvement: "You'll always get what you always got if you always do what you always did!" You must replace old habits with new habits. Everyone gets the same 24 hours in a day. People who are more successful simply have different habits from those who are less successful. What do you plan to do; what habits do you plan to develop in your 24 hours that speak directly to building your financial strength? What muscles will help you develop new habits? The true measure of your values results from what you practice rather than what you say. What you do authenticates your success!

God grants us the ability to obtain both spiritual and finacial strength which helps us achieve peace. This little book will assist you in your adventure in faith.

ENJOY!

You will keep on getting what you're getting if you keep on doing what you're doing.
Les Brown

"Let the Lord be magnified which has pleasure in the prosperity of His servant."
(Psalms 35:27)

The right frame of mind... Positive Thinking

"I can do all things through Christ which strengthens me."
Phillipians 4:13

1. Start with the right frame of mind, self-talk; this will produce the results you want. You will do what you think about!

2. Tell yourself over and over that with God's grace you have the power to make spiritual and financial strength happen for you.

The greatest thing in the world is
not so much where we start as in
what direction we're moving.
Oliver Wendell Holmes

"Beloved, I wish above all things
that you may prosper and be in health,
even as your soul prospers"
(John 2:3)

"For unto eveyone who has shall be given
in abundance; but you who have not shall be
taken away even that which you have."
(Matthew 25:29)

3. Right now, WRITE your top three financial goals in concrete terms - specific, achievable, and with deadlines.

GOAL   DEADLINE

a.
_____

b.
_____

c.
_____

Right now, write your top three spiritual goals that will support achieving your financial goals.

a.
_____

b.
_____

c.
_____

7

We must learn money management.
It is unAmerican not to!
Thomas & Kimberly Hines Bullock

"The blessing of the Lord, it makes us rich,
and He adds no sorrow with it."
(Proverbs 10:2)

4. Convince yourself that you deserve financial strength!

5. Develop a prayer that supports your belief; a prayer that helps you to become a faithful steward over your finances. Write your prayer now.

_____
_____
_____

6. Build money muscle-financial strength the same way you build body muscle-physical strength. Positive mental energy plus focused behaviors give you the results you want.

7. Build savings through automatic deductions. Add raises and bonuses to your automatic deductions.

> "The better you manage your money, the more money comes your way."
> Dwight Nichols,
> author of *God's Plans for Your Finances.*

Everybody, absolutely everybody,
can save money.
Michael East

"A prudent person foresees the difficulties
ahead and prepares for them; the simpleton
goes blindly on and suffers the consequences."
(Proverbs 22:3)

"Moreover, it is required in stewards,
that you be found faithful."
(Corinthians 4:2)

Frugality...

*"There is treasure to be desired and oil in the dwelling of the wise;
but a foolish person spend it up."*
Proverbs 21:20

8. Spend less, especially on consumable products! Start right now by spending 10% less!

9. Discipline yourself to spend less on. EVERYTHING.

10. Never buy retail and if you must shop...

11. Shop garage sales.

12. Shop liquidation sales.

We must get and remain serious
about financial planning. Period!
Earl G. Graves, Sr.
Publisher, Black Enterprise

When your month outlasts your money, you're in
serious stress.
Drs. Leroy and Johnnie Miles

"Honor the Lord your substance, and
with the first fruits of your increase."
(Proverbs 3:9)

13. Shop at auctions (if you know what you are doing! If not, learn.)

14. Shop at pawn shops.

15. Shop at thrift stores, flea markets, resale and consignment stores.

16. Buy "used" or "pre-owned" (whichever sounds better...used if the car is under $20,000... pre-owned if over $20,000).

17. Shop the want ads and trade papers.

Every penny counts.
Robert and Jackie Hines

Nobody gets to a dollar without
starting with a penny.
George E. Walker, Jr.
"Bubba"

"Any enterprise is built by wise planning,
becomes strong through common sense, and
profits wonderfully by keeping abreast of facts."
(Proverbs 24:3-4)

18. Shop credit union and bank repossessions.

19. Practice your assertive communication skills by asking salespeople to reduce items...all items. Ask for the manager. Say, "Please mark this down to a more reasonable price." Laugh out loud at prices!

20. Check out recordings and books from libraries (free!).

21. Use 800 numbers every chance you can. If you don't have the 800 number, call the central 800 directory.
(1-800-555-1212)

Accumulating money is so easy,
I'm surprised more people
aren't rich. That's the way money
works. The important thing is not how much money
a person makes, it is what he does with it that
matters.
A.P. Gaston

Stingy people, cheap
people, and people weak in faith – it's all the same.
They make me nervous.
Angela Walker

22. Insist on the lowest rate possible for hotels. Genuine complaints often generate even lower rates.

23. Wrap ALL! ALL! gifts in newspaper! Make your own cards or write notes.

24. Use coupons all the time.

25. Send for rebates all the time!

26. Limit your time in malls unless the stores are closed and you are exercising, or better yet, stay out of malls!. There are no "items of necessity" in a mall.

Anybody can be rich; all they have to do is want less.
Melva T. Walker "Nanny" and
George E. Walker, Sr. "Grandaddy"

"Riches and honor come from you alone,
and you are the ruler of all mankind; your
hand controls power and might, and it is
at your discretion that we are made
great and given strength."
(1Chronicles 29:12)

27. Eliminate shopping as a recreational activity. Instead, volunteer your time to help someone else. Join civic organizations or United Way groups like Big Brothers and Big Sisters. Work more actively in your church.

28. Buy grocery and household items in bulk through warehouse clubs. Pool and share bulk buys with neighbors, friends and family members.

29. When getting prescriptions, insist on free **samples.**

Everything is expensive, even a candy bar, when you are broke.
Elsie Hines

We could all do better than we are doing.
Carolyn Hines, Sr.
"Grandmommy"

"Where there is no vision, the people perish, but those who keep the law, happy are they.
(Proverbs 29:18)

30. Use generic prescription drugs.

31. Reduce or eliminate ATM use except for traceable emergencies. 80% of ATM withdrawals are untraceable. This practice also lowers your chances of getting mugged.

32. Make a budget and stick to it.

33. Practice the Pareto Rule. This 80-20 rule applies to all aspects of your life. If you own 20 blouses or shirts, 80% of the time you wear the same six, so why keep accumulating "stuff"?!

Economics do not dictate a
level of intelligence. However,
economics do dictate opportunity.
Bill Cosby

"And whatsoever you do, do it heartily."
(Colossians 3:23)

"The rich rules over the poor, and the
borrower is servant to the leader."
(Proverbs 22:7)

34. Buy checks through mail order. (Checks in the mail - 1-800-733-4333).

35. Mail order glasses, contact lenses and nylons.

36. Save 30-40% or even more on grocery costs by joining a wholesale food service.

37. Carry lunch to work. Spending just $5.00 a day on lunch amounts to $100.00 a month that could be saved and invested.

ALWAYS, ALWAYS, ALWAYS SPEND LESS THAN YOU EARN.

Be honest with yourself.
You know the dumb things
you are doing!
Frances Maclin Walker

Not poor, just broke.
Dick Gregory

"You become poor who deals with a
slack hand; but the hands of the
diligent become rich."
(Proverbs 10:4)

38. Install ceiling fans to save 10-15% on air-conditioning costs.

39. Cut your electric bills up to 40% by installing a load controller. Ask your power company.

40. Have a garage sale, offering little used, unused and mystery items from your attic, closets, drawers, basement and garage. Practice the Pareto Rule. Sell that stuff! Donate a percentage of the earnings to a charity.

41. Really...really shop air fares. Be flexible around departure and arrival times and locations. Could mean the difference of 40-50%. Plan to stay over a Saturday night. Watch the difference in fares. Press for discounts and specials.

It is great to be on cruise
control. You can't cruise unless
you work together.
Frank & Geraldine
Galloway

"Steady plodding brings prosperity; hasty
speculation brings poverty."
(Proverbs 21:5)

42. Cancel little used cable channels or cancel cable altogether.

43. Disconnect little used or unnecessary telephone charges. Do you really need caller I.D.?

44. Save-save-save through wholesale mail order. (Check the back of magazines.)

> *Our Lord rewards diligence.*

You are 100% responsible
for keeping your money!
Joe & Millicent
Harrison

"Train up a child in the way he should go and when he is old, he will not depart from it."
(Proverbs 22:6)

45. Buy all holiday and/or special gifts in January or at rock-bottom markdowns (75-80% off or more!). Give grocery items and staples for gifts.

46. Get better hotel rates by calling the hotel directly and insist on upgrades at reduced costs. Enroll in VIP programs in frequently used hotels.

47. If you absolutely have to have a new car, be ferocious. Do your homework and vow to pay no more than 4% over cost. Don't fall for rebates, delivery fees, etc.

Save...of course we do and
we make sure our brothers
and sisters save too!
Keith & Pat Andrews
Gene & Sheila Mason
Sandra Johnson Hines
Ernest, Clay, Christopher
& Barry Johnson
Gary and Samantha Johnson

"All good things come to those who
love the Lord; to those who are called to
His purpose."
(Romans 8:28)

48. Check out credit unions for rates on auto loans, also buying services, repossessions, pawn shops, etc.

49. Eliminate and/or reduce long distance costs by using email, writing, or phone cards. Give phone cards as gifts, especially to senior citizens and students.

50. Enroll in Upromise (Upromise.com) which allows a percentage of your spending to go directly into a college account for children.

It just makes sense to be
careful about money.
It's too hard to come by.
Elaine & Wesley
Wilson

"And God is able to make all grace
abound toward you; that you always
having all sufficiency in all things, may
abound to every good work."
(2Corinthians 9:8)

51. Bargain for everything!

- Hair cuts

- Medical services

- Groceries

- Gasoline

- All consumables

- Bargain

- Bargain

- Bargain

Just get started...
a little bit at a time.
Bob & Emily
Barnes

"Be willing and obedient and
eat the good of the land."
(Isaiah 1:19)

52. Grow (do) your own...

- Vegetables

- Grass

- Fruits

- Hair

- Herbs

- Exercise programs

- Fingernails

- Dry cleaning

- etc.

Faith, discipline and work- the core of everything.
Dominique & Reginald Hines

"Obey and serve the Lord, so you will spend your days in prosperity and your years in pleasures."
(Job 36:11)

53. Explore free entertainment. (Parks, college and university programs, libraries, etc.) Go to movies only at matineess.

54. Check your grocery bills. Scanners are often scammers!

55. When buying stocks, practice dollar cost averaging, investing the same amount each month and reinvest the dividends.

There's a penny, Grammy.
We gotta keep it! –
Symone Bullock

We pick up pennies. –
Kimberly Hines-Bullock
Michael Hines, J. Cecil
Sybil Walker-Mercer
Jenna Walker
Skip Walker

"The Lord desires above all things that
you may prosper and be in health, even as
your soul prospers."
(3 John 2)

56. If you know you can't afford the BMW, sell it and drive a Honda! Reduce your stress and model good sense!

57. Avoid service contracts on your cars. Avoid service contracts on everything - period!

58. Wash silks and other delicate fabrics with dishwashing liquid.

**Put it back!
You don't need it!
Ken & Maureen Booker**

**"For then God will make my
way prosperous, and then I will
have good success."
(Joshua 1:8)**

59. Shop for a new car at the end of the month.

60. Buy big ticket items when they are out of season.

61. Be assertive! Ask people who appear to know what they are doing about money. Would you ask an auto mechanic about laying bricks?

62. Shop street vendors and Bargain! Bargain! Bargain!

Not to disregard small amounts. If
you can save a dollar here and three dollars there,
it tends to add up. Don't under-estimate the power
of compound interest. If you manage to save $15 a
week either by bringing your lunch or sharing a ride
and invest that at 10 percent, after a while you'll
have thousands of dollars. I have done that in my
life, and it has really made a difference.
Humberto Cruz, writer of the
syndicated column "The Savings Game" and self-
made millionaire.

"The Lord my God teaches me to profit,
and leads me in the way that I should go."
(Isaiah 48:17)

Banking, Savings, Investments, Wills, Insurance, Trusts

"A good man leaves an inheritance to his children's children."
Proverbs 13:22

63. Pay yourself! First tithe, then make sure you are making maximum contributions to your 401k, profit-sharing or whatever plans you have access to.

64. Pay yourself second! Open an individual retirement account (IRA). Use payroll deductions, automatic bank drafts!

65. Pay yourself third! Make active investments in stocks, mutual funds via payroll deductions. These can be started for as little as $10.00 per month.

The first 2 letters of goal - GO!
So go now and act on your goals.
Dr. Deloris Saunders

Improperly set goals can act like anchors and weigh you down.
Dr. Violet Henighan

"The Lord has pleasure in my prosperity since I am His servant."
(Psalm 35:27)

66. Cut brokers fees by buying individual stocks yourself through National Association of Investment Clubs (NAIC) or directly through the companies in which you want to invest. Research carefully.

67. Establish and keep current your wills and trust. Review yearly.

68. Apply for your bank's private banking program where you are treated as a VIP and fees really are reduced or not paid at all. If your bank does not have one, change banks.

69. When selecting a mutual fund, focus on the fund's consistency rather than last year's performance; no loads.

**You are never too old or too young
to invest. You only need to get going!
Jann Alexander
Bennie & Josephine Spencer**

**"I seek the Lord, so I will not
lack any good thing."
(Psalm 34:10)**

70. If you are self-employed, establish a KEOGH or SEP-IRA. Contribute at the maximum levels possible.

71. Understand insurance and buy what you need. Remember long-term health care. (A MUST!)

72. Buy stocks that DRIP (dividend reinvestment plans) which automatically reinvest shareholder's dividends.

73. Maximize your child's eligibility for financial aid by keeping assets in your tax-deferred accounts.

**Increase savings, reduce spending.
Jason Bonner**

**"I am faithful, so I will abound with blessings."
(Proverbs 28:20)**

74. Ask (demand) your bank to waive overdrawn check fees.

75. Vow to start - next month - buying at least one share of stock in a company you really know.

76. If you're nervous about getting started in the stock market, consider starting with your utility company or a single share in a blue chip company.

77. Contribute the maximum to your company sponsored pension plan. Always do this. We repeat - ALWAYS!

When you pay cash,
you know the true cost.
Michael Hines

"I am faithful, so I will
abound with blessings."
(Proverbs 28:20)

Credit Cards, Mortgages, Taxes, Insurance

"Owe no man anything, but to love one another: for he that loves another has fulfilled the law."
Romans 13:8

78. Prepay your mortgage principal by a fixed amount each month. As little as $25.00 per month makes a heck of a difference. Own Real Estate!

79. Own and use only one charge card with an interest rate of 7% or less. Credit card debt is utterly foolish.

80. Stay out of department stores. Absolutely no store credit cards!

> ## CREDIT CARDS...
> ## INSTRUMENTS OF SATAN!
> ### William & Carolyn Hines

Plastic breaks...
don't let it break you!
James & Geraldine
Woodley

"I do not grow weary in doing good; therefore, in due season I will reap, if I do not give up."
(Galatians 6:9)

81. If you currently carry credit card balances, press your issuer to reduce the interest to the lowest level available. Be persistent.

82. Cancel all credit cards that have annual fees. Ask for any and all discounts.

83. Review your credit report and close (purge) unused accounts. Now!

Never pay the minimum; at least double your payments, or better yet, don't charge it in the first place!
Dee & Valerie Ellis

"I delight in the Lord, and He will give me the desires of my heart."
(Psalm 37:4)

84. If you must use credit cards, use one that awards perks. Remember that perks are seldom free! Perks are not the sole determining factor in selecting a credit card. Pay close attention to the financial terms of the offer.

85. Review the exemptions on your W-4 and take the money instead of letting Uncle Sam use it all year.

86. Look for all insurance discounts, non-smoking, anti-theft, senior citizens, fire-resistance features, etc.

You may not get all you pay for in
this world, but you most certainly pay for all you get.
Frederick Douglass

Lord, I got to work! Broke is no fun!
Vertis Johnson

"The blessings of the Lord make me rich,
and He adds no sorrow to them."
(Proverbs 10:22)

87. Do not purchase or keep unnecessary insurance coverage like private mortgage insurance, insurance on children under 18, maintenance agreements, etc. (Call the Insurance Information Institute at 1-800-942-4242).

88. Negotiate with credit card issuers for (a) lower consumer loan rates; (b) mortgages; (c) combined balances. Negotiate for everything!

89. Consider using a managed health care plan which could cost 15-20% less than traditional insurance (group Health Association of America at 202-778-3268).

You don't need three, five or
ten credit cards to function – even in our plastic
society. You only "need" one, given the wide
acceptance of most cards. Count 'em up, including
retail store and gas cards, and get rid of 'em.
Eric Tyson

"I do not fear, for it is my God's good
pleasure to give me the Kingdom."
(Luke 13:32)

90. When restoring your credit, inform potential lenders of any glitches in your credit report before making your application.

91. Avoid buying term life insurance on children. Consider investing the money in a mutual fund gift trust, or education funds, etc.

92. Eliminate all credit card debt as quickly as possible, and better yet, avoid accumulating credit card debt!

93. Ask people to give you money, stocks, or bonds for gifts and to do the same for your children. You model the way by doing the same for others.

"Dear Lord, help to free
us all from credit card debt."
Dr. Erma Freeman

"God is doing...all that I ask or think,
according to the power that works in me."
(Ephesians 3:20)

94. Use free budget counseling (24 hour toll free line) from the Consumer Credit Counseling Service (800-388-2227).

95. Study, study, study! Ask, ask, ask!

96. Avoid insurance cancellations by raising your deductible to $500 or $1,000.

97. Vow to file your taxes on time. Paying penalties is stupid-foolish-dumb-asinine! April 15th comes the same time every year! DUH!

When you use a credit card and
you don't have the money, it is not too far from
stealing.
Granddaddy told me that.
Jenna Walker

"God has given to me all things
that pertain to life and godliness, through
the knowledge of Him who has called
me to glory and virtue."
(2 Peter 1:3)

98. Interview people who seem "to get it" and follow their advice.

99. When buying a house in a development, by-pass the realtor, deal directly with the developer.

Do leave home without it!
Erik and Adrienne Cooper

"Faith without works is dead."
(James 2:17)

Money, Friends and Family

"Train up a child in the way he should go; and when he is old, he will not depart from it."
Proverbs 22:6

100. Give people, especially students and newlyweds, money, MONEY!-STOCKS-CHECKS-CASH-BOOKS for all gifts.

101. When you loan a family member or friend money, consider it a gift. They rarely pay you back so considering the loan a gift saves you considerable stress. If you insist, draw up official loan papers showing all terms and conditions of the loan. Be prepared to garnish their wages or write it off as a bad debt.

102. Encourage your child to earn a bachelor's degree in less than four years. Community colleges are excellent bargains for the first two years toward the bachelor's degree.

Students have gotten hooked on plastic and are racking up huge
debts that will plague them for years.
Joseph P. Kennedy

"The crown of the wise is their riches,
but the foolishness of fools is folly."
(Proverbs 14:24)

103. Make a date to seriously discuss money matters with your significant others. Then do it!!! Make this a regular practice.

104. Share personal stories of money tips (successes and flubs, include horror stories!)

105. Start an investment club with friends or family members (go on line and research this area!).

When you loan money to
someone, think immediately
that it is a gift. This saves you
stress. - Dr. Violet Walker Henighan

Family is one thing.
Business is another.
Beverly Brewer

"I give and it will be given to me.
Good measure, pressed down, shaken
together, and running over will be given to me."
(Luke 6:12)

Common Sense - Health & Wealth

"Every prudent man deals with knowledge; but a fool lays open his folly."
Proverbs 13:16

106. Quit All unhealthy, costly habits like smoking and drinking.

107. Use free services for recreation.

108. Eliminate or reduce spa or health club expenses by using the "Y", a workout program at home or simply walking/jogging.

Let's share information,
all the information we
can with family and friends.
Dr. John and Clevonne Turner

"Jesus came so that we might
have life, and that we might have life
more abundantly."
(John 10:10)

109. Consider using ambulatory care centers - saving as much as 20-50% for outpatient and/or emergency room services. To find one close to you, call National Association for Ambulatory Care 305-441-2421.

110. Require children to work, and then require them to save half of their earnings.

111. Use DIAL-A-NURSE (1-800-535-1111) as much as possible for free health information.

112. Buy software directly from the manufacturer.

**If you hang around two broke people,
you will be the third!
James "Skip" and Erika Walker**

**"The wealth of the sinner is laid up
for the just." (Proverbs 13:22)**

113. If you must purchase software buy bundled packages.

114. Change your opinions about retirement. Keep working even though you may be convinced you're supposed to retire. Think re-career rather than retire. People are living longer and healthier, better quality lives.

Work together, save together,
plan together, play together,
pray together.
William and Carolyn Hines

"This book of the law will not depart
out of (our) mouths, but (we) will meditate
on it day and night, that (we) may observe to do
according to all that is written in it. For then
God will make (our) way prosperous, and then
(we) will have good success."
(Joshua 1:8)

Start Your Own Business

"Not slothful in business; fervent in spirit; serving the Lord."
Romans 12:11

115. Think small business. Inventory your talents and sell your services. Consider everything. Here are a few:

A. Specialty dishes (catering).

B. Party support

C. Calligraphy

D. House sitting

E. Yard care

All the money in the world
doesn't mean a thing if you don't have time
to enjoy it.
Oprah Winfrey

"My God will supply all my needs
according to His riches in glory
by Christ Jesus."
(Phillippians 4:19)

F. Dog (pet) sitting

G. Child care; elder care

H. Plant care

I. Manicures, pedicures, etc.

J. Sewing, crafts, upholstery

K. Art-works

L. All forms of hobbies

M. Writing; word processing; researching

N. Driving, delivery

O. Telephoning

P. Musical talent; lessons of all kinds

At the bottom of education, at
the bottom of politics, even at the bottom of
religion, there must be economic independence.
Booker T. Washington

"I seek first the kingdom of God and His
righteousness, so all these things will be
added to me." (Matthew 6:33)

Q. Tapes; recordings

R. Running garage sales

S. Washing cars

T. Seminars; workshops; training

U. Franchising

V. Car detailing

W. Special events

X. Cleaning; maintenance

Y. Any and all forms of providing personal services

A. Selling goods, etc.

Just put it away for a rainy day 'cause it is going to rain.
Wes & Elaine Wilson

"And now, Lord, you are God, and have promised this goodness to your servant."
(1 Chronicles 17:26)

116. If you decide to start your own business, do your homework. There is no such thing as too much preparation. Use free business assistance services from the Chamber of Commerce, government assistance centers, community colleges and universities, and the Small Business Administration.

117. Accumulate loose change in a jar, deposit contents every two months.

118. Stop buying bottled water, especially since this is an unregulated industry. Get a water filter that fits your faucet and if it makes you feel better, tap your own water into one of those "chi-chi" bottles. Put your own label on the bottle.

Determine how you want
to get to where you want to go,
put your hands in God's hands,
and your plan is in gear!
Joyce Boisson

"For I know the plans I have for you says
the Lord. They are plans for good, not for
evil, to give you hope and a future, to prosper
you. In those days when you pray, I will listen.
If you look for me in the ernest,
you will find me when you seek me."
(Jeremiah 29:11-12)

119. Cut energy costs even more by looking for the Energy Star labels when you replace old appliances and electronic items.

120. Review your credit cards and transfer balances to lower card rates. Make this a regular practice.

121. Change your internet provider to NetZero or a low cost provider.

122. Eat in more often and make meal times relaxing and fun by focusing on how much money you are saving. When you eat out, split meals.

It's time to take charge of your life
or it will certainly take charge of you.
Wesley Wilson, Sr., age 94

We love the Lord.
The Hines and Walker Families

"Good understanding gains favor, but
the way of the unfaithful is hard."
(Proverbs 13:15)

Heed the advice of those who seem to
understand and live by God's word.
"Glory to God!"
Jim Walker

Food For Thought

"Let the whole earth sing to the Lord. Each day proclaim the good news that He saves."
1 Chronicles 16:23

"A race which cannot save its earnings can never rise in the scale of civilization."

– Frederick Douglass

"Politics doesn't control the world, money does. And we ought not to be upset about that. We ought to begin to understand how money works and why money works...if you want to bring about...feeding the hungry, clothing the naked, healing the sick - it's going to be done in the free market system. You need capital."

– Andrew Young

"Retiring at 65 is strictly an arbitrary idea, but it sticks in so many people's minds that they assume working after that age constitutes some kind of abuse of privilege. It really is ridiculous."

– Denton Cooley, Renowned Cardiovascular Surgeon

"We must tell people how little we pay for something, not how much."

– James "Skip" Walker, Jr.

"What you commit yourself to think and do determine who you are."

– Dr. Violet Henighan

"Work with all your might and all your mind."

– Matthew Mercer

"The real enjoyment of working comes when you know you don't have to work."

– Valarie Ellis

"Remember to share with God and others."

– Joanne Jenkins

"Remember, if you see a penny on the ground, bend over and pick it up…there may be a quarter nearby."

– William A. Hines, Jr.

Read - Read - Read
   Study - Study - Study
       Share - Share - Share

> "Give, and it shall be given unto you; good measure, pressed down, and shaken together, and running over, shall come into your bosom. For with the same measure that you mete it shall be measured to you again."
> Luke 6:38

The Guerrilla Guide to Credit Repair: How to find out what is wrong with your credit rating and how to fix it.
by Todd Bierman and Nathaniel Wice

Resources Overdrawn, Under Deposited.
by Beverlee Kelley

"Age Discrimination on the Job" (Free)
American Association of Retired Persons
D'12386, P.O. Box 22796, Long Beach, CA 90801

American Association of Franchises and Dealers
(800-733-9858)

American Franchise Association (800-334-4232)

American Society of Home Inspectors
(800-743-2744) (check new home construction)

"Automotive News" (nearby library) (scrutinize rebates, dealer incentives, best prices)

The Bank Book: How to Revoke Your Bank's License to Steal (800-242-7737)

Bankcard Holders of America (updated list of best credit card deals. "Credit Cards: What You Don't Know Can Cost You.") 524 Branch Drive, Salem, VA 24153

"The Banker's Secret Bulletin" (newsletter for cheapskates)
Good Advice Press, Box 78, Elizaville, NY 12523

Black Enterprise

"Bottom Line Personal" (800-274-5611) P.O. Box 58446, Boulder, CO 80322

Car Bargains (800-475-7283) (Car pricing service)

"Cheapskate Monthly" (small practical ways to cut costs and end annual spending) Box 2135, Paramount, CA 90723

"Cheap Tricks: 100's of Ways You Can Save 1000's of Dollars" (cheap solutions to help with high cost of consumer items)

"Consumer Guide to Comprehensive Financial Planning" (free) (to select your financial planner) International Association for Financial Planning (800-945-4237)

"Consumer Guide to Home Energy Savings" (510-549-9914) (tips on how to slash utility bills)

Courage to be Rich, Suze Orman

CUNA Public Relations (to join a credit union) P.O. Box 431, Madison, WV 53701

Credit Bureau Addresses:
    TRW, P.O. Box 2350, Dallas, TX 75374
    Trans Union, P.O. Box 740241, Atlanta, GA 30374
    Equifax, P.O. Box 740241, Atlanta, GA 30374 (800-685-1111)

Department of Housing and Urban Development's Hotline (800-669-9777)
(if racial bias encountered when seeking home loan)

"Export Programs" (free) International Trade Administration (800-872-8723)
(trade shows, market research and financing)

"Family Business Advisor" (800-551-0633)

Federal Reserve System (guide for selecting credit cards)
Publication Services, MS-127, Washington, DC 20551

"$Frugal Connoisseur", P.O. Box 290-183, Waterford, MI 48329
(a guide for cost cutting)

Group Health Association of America (202-778-3258) (to find managed CU program)

Institute of Certified Financial Planners (800-282-7526) (to select financial planner)

International Reciprocal Trade Association (to find barter groups for disposing of excess inventory) 9513 Beach Mill Road, Great Falls, VA 22066

The Joy of Outlet Shopping (a guide to outlet stores and centers with free coupons)

"Money Guide: Best College Buys" (to choose top-notch public college)
P.O. Box 30626, Tampa, FL 33630

National Association for Ambulatory Care (305-441-2421 or phone book)
(to find nearby ambulatory care center)

The National Association of Enrolled Agents (800-424-4339) (to help with your taxes)

National Business Coalition on Health (NBCH) (202-775-9300) (to help small firms to provide health insurance)

OPRAH

"The Penny Pincher" (newsletter for cheapskates)
P.O. Box 809, Kings Park, NY 11754

RAM Research (updated list of best credit card deals) Box 1700, Frederick, MD 21702

Securities and Exchange Commission, Washington, DC
(To check record of financial planner)

"The Sensible Saver" (Includes grocery coupon book)
7948 Wornall Road, #1237, Kansas City, MO 64114

"Skinflint News" (800-469-8672) P.O. Box 818, Palm, Harbor, FL 34682

Small Business Development Centers / Small Business Administration
(Information on exporting your products)

"Socially Responsible Investing" by Alan Miller from NY Institute of Finance

Telecommunications Research and Action Center
P.O. Box 12038, Washington, DC 20005 (Send a self-addressed, stamped envelope to receive rate comparisons for five of the biggest long-distance carriers)

"The Ultimate Credit Handbook" (800-255-0899) (credit card management)

"Think and Grow Rich, A Black Choice," Kimbro, Dennis (available in libraries and major book stores)

Working Assets Money Market Portfolio (800-223-7010) (if interested in investing in companies that create jobs, finance moderate income housing, etc.)

"Glory to God"
Jimmy Walker

FOR ADDITIONAL COPIES PLEASE WRITE, CALL OR FAX:

C.W. HINES and ASSOCIATES, INC.
344 Churchill Circle
Santuary Bay
White Stone, VA 22578
(804) 435-8844   Fax: (804) 435-8855
E-mail: turtlecwh@aol.com
Web Page: cwhinesassociates.org

Notes

Notes